WRITE YOUR OWN

SCIENCE FICTION

STORY

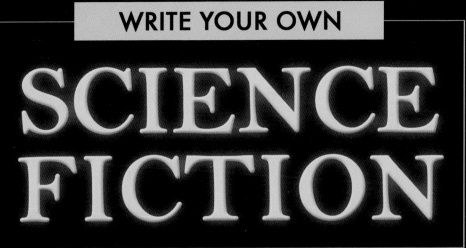

by Tish Farrell

First published in the United States in 2006 by
Compass Point Books
3109 West 50th Street #115
Minneapolis, MN 55410

Copyright © ticktock Entertainment Ltd 2006
First published in Great Britain in 2006 by ticktock Media Ltd.,
ISBN 1 86007 532 0 PB

Visit Compass Point Books on the Internet at
www.compasspointbooks.com
or e-mail your request to
custserv@compasspointbooks.com

For Compass Point Books:
Sue Vander Hook, Nick Healy, Anthony Wacholtz, Nathan Gassman, James Mackey, Abbey Fitzgerald, Catherine Neitge, Keith Griffin, and Carol Jones

For ticktock Entertainment Ltd
Graham Rich, Elaine Wilkinson, John Lingham,
Suzy Kelly, Heather Scott, Jeremy Smith

Library of Congress Cataloging-in-Publication Data
Farrell, Tish.
  Write your own science fiction story / by Tish Farrell.
      p. cm. — (Write your own)
  Includes bibliographical references and index.
  Audience: Grades 4-6.
  ISBN-13: 978-0-7565-1643-7 (hardcover)
  ISBN-10: 0-7565-1643-9 (hardcover)
  ISBN-13: 978-0-7565-1818-9 (paperback)
  ISBN-10: 0-7565-1818-0 (paperback)
  1. Science fiction—Authorship—Juvenile literature. I. Title. II. Series.
  PN3377.5.S3F37 2006
  808.3'8762—dc22   2005030732

Your writing mission

Artificial intelligence, genetic engineering, probes on Mars—where is our technology taking us? To a sun-bright future or the collapse of civilization? If questions like these fire your imagination, then learn how to turn them into captivating science-fiction stories. This book cannot transport you to another galaxy, but it will help you to write beyond the limits of the known world. To help you on your way, there will be a variety of training and brainstorming exercises that will develop your creative writing skills. There will also be examples from famous science-fiction writers to inspire you.

CONTENTS

LEARN TO BE A WRITER

If you want to be a writer, this book is the perfect place to start. It aims to give you the tools to write your own science-fiction stories. Learn how to craft believable characters and perfect plots, along with satisfying beginnings, middles, and endings. Examples from famous books appear throughout, with tips and techniques from published authors to help you on your way.

Get the writing habit

Do timed and regular practice. Real writers learn to write even when they don't particularly feel like it.

Create a story-writing zone.

Keep a journal.

Keep a notebook—record interesting events and note how people behave and speak.

Generate ideas

Find a character whose story you want to tell. What is his or her problem?

Brainstorm to find out everything about your character.

Research settings, events, and other characters.

Get a mix of good and evil characters.

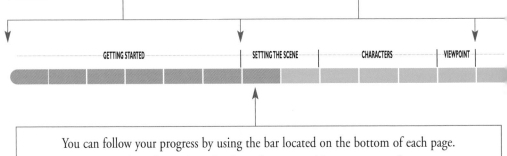

GETTING STARTED   SETTING THE SCENE   CHARACTERS   VIEWPOINT

You can follow your progress by using the bar located on the bottom of each page.
The orange color tells you how far along the story-writing process you have gotten.
As the blocks are filled out, your story will be growing.

Plan

What is your story about?

What happens?

Plan beginning, middle, and end.

Write a synopsis or create story-boards.

Write

Write the first draft, then put it aside for a while.

Check spelling and dialogue—does it flow?

Remove unnecessary words.

Does the story have a good title and satisfying ending?

Avoid clichés.

Publish

Write or print the final draft.

Always keep a copy for yourself.

Send your story to literary magazines, Internet writing sites, competitions, or school magazines.

SYNOPSES AND PLOTS | WINNING WORDS | SCINTILLATING SPEECH | HINTS AND TIPS | THE NEXT STEP

When you get to the end of the bar, your book is ready to go! You are an author!
You now need to decide what to do with your book and what your next project should be.
Perhaps it will be a sequel to your story, or maybe something completely different.

BEGIN YOUR QUEST

While real-life scientists need high-tech laboratories and expensive research programs to conduct their experiments, science-fiction writers only need a pen, some paper, and their imagination. They need a good library, too, or access to the Internet to explore the latest scientific ideas that might inspire new stories.

Gather what you need

As you follow the advice in this book, you may find that some of the following will help you organize your creative efforts:

- A small notebook that you carry everywhere
- Pencils and pens with brightly colored ink
- Different colored Post-it notes to mark any ideas during your research
- Stick-on stars to highlight your best ideas
- Folders for all bits of useful research and your brainstorming exercises to refer to later
- A dictionary
- A thesaurus
- An encyclopedia
- A computer or word processor

Find your writing place

You will need a special writing place. Again, writers are lucky. They can work where they choose. Roald Dahl (author of *Charlie and the Chocolate Factory* and many other books) turned his garden shed into his special creative zone. You could make your bedroom your center of operations. Or perhaps your local Internet café or library has just the right atmosphere.

Create a story-writing zone

• Play the right music to spark those story ideas.

• Put up a poster showing Earth from space or a selection of high-tech images that especially intrigue you.

• Put on a hat or scarf that you only wear when you're writing.

• Gather some mysterious objects to inspire your spirit of inquiry—a rock or a fossil that you found (evidence of some alien life-form?).

Spend time choosing these things. Your writing place is important—special things are going to happen there.

Follow the writer's golden rule

Once you have chosen your writing space, the first step in becoming a writer is: Go there as often as possible and write. You must write and write regularly. This is the writer's golden rule.

Until you are ready, no writing can happen. It doesn't matter what you write—an e-mail or a diary entry will do—as long as you write something.

Before astronauts head for the stars, they must undergo long training programs to prepare them for conditions in space. Becoming a writer is like this. Don't just write when you feel like it. If all writers did this, there would be far fewer books on the planet.

Now it's your turn

Unlock your imagination

Try this brainstorming exercise. Have pens and scrap paper ready, plus a timer. Then sit quietly in your writing zone for a few moments. Set the timer for two minutes and write the phrase "space-time continuum" at the top of the paper. Now, without taking the pen from the page, write all the science-fiction words, phrases, and names you can think of. Don't worry about spelling or if any of it makes sense. Then stop when two minutes are up. You've taken a first step toward creating your own world in fiction.

MARTIAN
SPACEMAN

KRYPTONITE
METEOR
ALIEN

Now it's your turn

Describe your fictional world

Take five of your favorite brainstormed words from the previous exercise. Set the timer for 10 minutes and write a description of another world you'd most like to visit. Include your five chosen words. Is it a faraway planet? Your hometown a thousand years from now? A space lab? Already you are finding ways to mine the hidden depths of your imagination.

TIPS AND TECHNIQUES

Keep all your brainstorming notes in a file or notebook. You will need them later. Don't let a Martian invasion or approaching asteroids stop your writing practice. Set a time slot and stick to it.

Case study

When sci-fi writer Robert J. Sawyer (right) was in high school, he started a sci-fi addicts club. With fellow members, he wrote scripts for a radio drama series that was never made. Later, Sawyer cut out all ideas that hadn't been his and shaped his first publishable story called "Motive." Many of the ideas in this first story—a murderous computer and dinosaur-like aliens—were developed in his later books, including his first novel, **Golden Fleece.**

Before you can write science fiction, you need to know what it is. In libraries and bookstores, you will usually find sci-fi and fantasy books side by side. Both genres are called speculative fiction because they are set in imagined worlds that could not exist.

What is science fiction?

Science fiction spins real scientific facts and ideas into imaginative tales. These stories can show readers life in a future world or in another world altogether. Science-fiction writers can send their characters on travels through time or space. They can pit characters against the forces of evil, and they can show us the dangers and wonders the future may hold.

Science fiction vs. fantasy

Fantasy worlds are usually governed by magic. The stories show forces of good and evil trying to overcome each other's powers. Storytellers must state their own magic rules before they develop their tale.

In science fiction, the imagined worlds also have rules, but they are based on known scientific principles, which are often stretched to further development. For example, science fiction takes what we know about space travel and builds on it, making it possible for characters to visit faraway galaxies.

Read, read, read

Reading other writers' works will help develop your own special interests and make it easier for you to discover what you really want to write about. Try to read different types of science fiction.

Start with some of the classic writers—maybe H. G. Wells, Jules Verne, Isaac Asimov, or Ursula K. Le Guin. As you read them, look for the kinds of story ideas that excite you most.

TIPS AND TECHNIQUES

When thinking up your own stories, watch out for clichés. A cliché is an idea that has been used too often before. Like Klingon attacks, they are best avoided.

Take notes

As you read, keep a science-fiction log. Write down what books you have read and briefly say what they were about and why you did or did not enjoy them. Characters might start forming in your mind. Make notes, do drawings, and start a character collection. You will need them later.

Some of the great sci-fi themes

- alien invasions—H. G. Wells' *The War of the Worlds*
- robots and androids—Isaac Asimov's Robot series
- time travel—H. G. Wells' *The Time Machine*
- monsters out of place and time—Jules Verne's *Journey to the Centre of the Earth*
- virtual reality gone too far—Alan Gibbons' *Shadow of the Minotaur*
- life on other planets—Ursula K. Le Guin's *The Left Hand of Darkness*
- space exploration—Star Trek series
- space wars—Orson Scott Card's *Ender's Game*
- our world in the future—M. T. Anderson's *Feed*
- humorous science fiction—Terry Pratchett's Discworld series

Now it's your turn

Operation brainstorm

Think "outer space." In a two-minute timed practice, jot down as many different words you can think of to describe it—empty, void, black, airless? Does it have sounds and smells? What would they be?

The more you read, the more you will learn about writing, but you must have your writer's eye switched on first. As you read, ask questions. How does the writer make the story's world and characters convincing? How did the author build suspense or make the story's ending satisfying?

Finding your writer's voice

Once you start reading as a writer, you will notice that each story has its own rhythm and range of language that stays the same throughout the book. You will get to know different writers' styles. H.G. Wells is worlds apart from Douglas Adams, and Orson Scott Card writes very differently from Ursula K. Le Guin. In other words, you will discover their distinctive voices, ones that you can often recognize in much the same way that you know your favorite rock band when you hear their new song on the radio.

Experiment

Once you've found an author whose books you really enjoy, it can be tempting to stick to them. But at least now and then, read something quite different—a historical novel or a book of legends. You may be surprised what ideas it gives you.

Case study

Alan Gibbons, author of Shadow of the Minotaur, *got the writing bug from reading. He says, "I don't see how you can be a good writer without being a good reader."*

WRITERS' VOICES

Look at the kinds of words these writers use. Do they use many adjectives or long sentences? Are they convincing? Which style do you prefer to read?

ARTHUR C. CLARKE

It was the last days of the Empire. The tiny ship was far from home, and almost a hundred light-years from the great parent vessel searching through the loosely packed stars at the rim of the Milky Way. But even here it could not escape from the shadow that lay across civilization.

Arthur C. Clarke, "Encounter at Dawn"

PHILIP REEVE

Hester Shaw was starting to get used to being happy. After all her muddy, starveling years in the ditches and scavenger-villes of the Great Hunting Ground she had finally found herself a place in the world. She had her own airship, the Jenny Haniver.

Philip Reeve, *Predator's Gold*

DOUGLAS ADAMS

Zaphod Beeblebrox, President of the Imperial Intergalactic Government, sped across the seas of Damogran, his ion drive delta boat winking and flashing in the Damogran sun.

Douglas Adams, *The Hitchhiker's Guide to the Galaxy*

JAMES VALENTINE

Again, Jules was amazed at Gen's ability to keep up with all this. He was still being distracted by Theodore's hair, which was now a broad stripe of yellow with red and green lightning bolts flashing on either side, and whenever the time travel stuff came up he could feel the entire concept slipping away from him, like most of what his math teacher said.

James Valentine, the Jumpman series

H. G. WELLS

The living intelligence, the Martian within the hood, was slain and splashed to the four windows of heaven, and the thing was now a mere intricate device of metal whirling to its destruction.

H. G. Wells, *The War of the Worlds*

Science-fiction writers usually explore big ideas in their stories—the end of civilization as we know it, for example. The imagined crises they describe challenge us to think about our lives now and wonder how things might be in the future.

Find big ideas

Writers are continually absorbing information about subjects that interest them. Their data-gathering minds are always on full alert, whether they are watching TV or chatting with friends, even when they are asleep. They make notes and read everything that might spark an idea or develop their knowledge.

Case study

Lois Lowry's father lost most of his long-term memory due to illness. One day, after visiting him in the nursing home, she realized that without memory, there is no pain. She began to imagine a society in which the past was deliberately forgotten, and from this idea, she wrote The Giver.

Gather material

Your subconscious mind is probably already full of story ideas—the books you've read, the films you've watched, and all those episodes of *The X-Files*. It is only in your conscious mind that you forget these things. To write your own stories, you need to access all that creative stuff in your subconscious mind. Brainstorming and asking what-if questions are good ways to start.

Case study

Orson Scott Card says he was 16 when he first thought of the setting for Ender's Game. *Warfare was on his mind because his older brother was in the military. One day, as he was being driven to school, he began to wonder: What sort of training would soldiers need for space combat? The answer came: a battle school in space, where child recruits could be trained for a space war against alien invaders.*

Now it's your turn

Brainstorm

Today, you discovered you were an android, the only one in your family. Ask yourself these questions: How did I discover it? How does it make me feel? Does it explain why I often feel different from everyone else, and if so, in what ways? Do I have some special talent that makes my schoolmates jealous? Now write for 20 minutes. If you think you have the makings of a good story, continue it.

TIPS AND TECHNIQUES

Brainstorm when you are bored or nervous—in your dentist's waiting room or while waiting to take a test. You may come up with your best ideas, and it takes your mind off everything. Make lists. How many ways can you describe yellow? How many metals can you think of? How dark is dark? How far is far? Tap the hidden depths of your imagination.

Having a story idea is just the start. Next comes much research while you develop the idea into a story. You will need some science facts and some real-world information to grow a good story.

Grow your idea

Start the gathering process. Write down any good ideas or interesting information in your notebook. Maybe you can use your own interests or special knowledge—of computer games, sports, astronomy, or anything—to develop a futuristic story.

TIPS AND TECHNIQUES

To develop the story of your life as an android (from page 15), you would need information on robotics and artificial intelligence. Start a file. Give it a name—Operation Android. Then read lots of stories that deal with these subjects. Watch good films and ask yourself: Are there any ideas here that will help me understand what being an android would be like?

Find facts

• Search for related articles in the media.

• Look for doom-and-gloom headlines.

• Look for direct quotes about awful or extraordinary things that have happened to people. Their words might trigger your own characters.

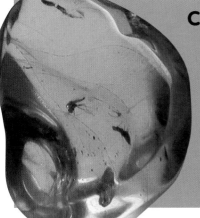

Case study

Canadian sci-fi writer Robert J. Sawyer uses **Science News** for his science facts. It was there that he read about prehistoric mosquitoes trapped in amber and the possibility of dinosaur blood being preserved in their bellies. The article raised the question of whether the blood could be used to clone dinosaurs. "Neat!" Sawyer thought and turned the page. When writer Michael Crichton read the same article, he thought "Yes!" It prompted him to write **Jurassic Park**.

- Search for more specialized articles in magazines or on media Web sites. CNN and PBS have good popular science coverage.

- Read science magazines: *Discover, Popular Science, National Geographic, Scientific American,* and so on.

TIPS AND TECHNIQUES

Start a dream diary to tap into your subconscious mind. Have a notebook beside your bed and write down any dream ideas as soon as you wake up.

Now it's your turn

Build worlds

Once your story ideas start simmering, you can help things along by building the physical world where your story will take place. Repeat the exercise on page 9. See if your fictional world has taken more shape. Can you feel your ideas developing? Do you need more?

MASTER YOUR UNIVERSE

The setting or imagined world in a sci-fi story is as important as the story itself. On his writing Web site, Robert J. Sawyer says, "One of the key skills for a sci-fi writer is world building—creating a convincing alternate reality."

Lay down the law

In the last chapter, you looked at ways to develop your story ideas by doing research. World building requires a similar process. The scientific laws that rule your world must work for your readers, so first ask yourself these questions.

- What are the rules in my world? Are there nights and days, seasons, or different climates? Is it natural or man-made? Is it Earth in the past or future?

- What are its colors, smells, and textures?

- What big disaster is looming—the loss of vital resources, an epidemic, or a war?

- Who will suffer most, and whose story is most important?

Build your world

World building is like writing a geography assignment and creating the geography, too. But you can use magazines, books, and computer games to imagine it better. Create a profile of your world. Draw maps and plans. Think yourself into it:

- What is there?

- How do people live and travel around?

- What are their houses like?

- What do people wear and eat?

- Are there aliens, robots, or thinking computers?

Now it's your turn

Brainstorm: It's a wonderful world

Read through your earlier brainstormed notes on an imagined world of your own creation (from pages 9 and 17). Pretend it's your job to attract new colonists to your sci-fi world. For 10 minutes, brainstorm some sales slogans to promote its attractions.

Next, write a different view in a diary account. This time, reveal your secret doubts about encouraging new settlers. When there are signs that things in your world aren't so good, why are your world's rulers so keen to attract newcomers? Take no more than 10 minutes. Don't think too hard—write top-of-your-head thoughts.

Case study

You don't always need an extraordinary setting for good science fiction. In Dinosaur Summer, Greg Bear sets the story in 1947 as a sequel to Arthur Conan Doyle's The Lost World. This was the first sci-fi dinosaur story, published in 1912, and in it, Doyle's character, Professor Challenger, discovers a population of surviving dinosaurs on a South American jungle plateau. Bear picks up the tale 35 years later. It is a good example of a writer building on an existing story without copying it.

TIPS AND TECHNIQUES

In a good sci-fi story, your characters' world will always be under some major threat. Check out science and space reports on news Web sites. The headlines could spark a tale. You may find strange stories, such as "Woman 'tastes' musical notes" and "Hidden galaxies spotted."

New writers find world building very absorbing. Some try to invent a new language with extraordinary names for everything they have created. This can make life too hard for readers. Instead, focus on how your world works and how its amazing aspects will affect your characters and their story.

Make your setting real

To make your setting real for readers, you need to trigger their senses. You can do this in different ways:

- Straight description. Tell the reader what it's like.

- Your characters' direct experiences. Show the reader what it is like.

- Analogies. Compare your world to a place your readers know.

Most people have never been in zero gravity, but Orson Scott Card finds a common human experience to describe his battleroom:

They filed clumsily into the battleroom, like children in a swimming pool for the first time, clinging to the handholds along the side. They soon found that things went better if they didn't use their feet at all.
Orson Scott Card, *Ender's Game*

What's the threat?

Whatever is threatening your world, it will affect the way you describe your setting. Look again at the opening of the Arthur C. Clarke story on page 13. See how it tells you where you are and combines action (traveling through space) with an instant sense of foreboding: "the shadow that lay across civilization."

Now your sci-fi world should be taking shape, and you have a good crisis lurking, so it's time to find out who your characters are.

TIPS AND TECHNIQUES

A key storytelling skill is to say just enough to move the story forward, while hinting that there is much more still to find out. If your world needs a lot of explaining, try putting the main details in a prologue—an introduction. Write it from the perspective of one of your characters.

Now it's your turn

A dramatic opening

Write an opening scene of about 200 words. Take 10 minutes. Combine setting details with some piece of action—maybe your hero arriving. Try adding a hint of doom, too. Choose the most descriptive verbs you can think of. For example, a starship doesn't just fly, it speeds through space. Similarly, a power plant throbs with pent-up energy, and a red sun looms through the solar dust.

DISCOVER YOUR HERO

Your hero or heroes (protagonists) are the lead actors in your story. You must care about them deeply and make readers feel the same way. Think of them as new friends. Sometimes they will surprise you.

Find a hero

Sci-fi films and books have marvelous heroes to inspire you. You can use them as role models and mix them with people you know. Will your hero be like brave Princess Leia in the Star Wars series? Or what about the boy, David, in Steven Spielberg's film *A.I.*, who looks human but is really a humanoid robot longing to be a real boy? Ender in *Ender's Game* is a 6-year-old child prodigy who is being trained as a battle commander for a future space war.

Now it's your turn

Know your hero

If your hero hasn't yet taken shape, here's a way to help.

On a large sheet of paper, roughly map out a square of 36 boxes, six across the top, six down the side. Write these headings in the boxes down the side:

(1) physical appearance, (2) clothing, (3) behavior, (4) strengths, (5) failings, and (6) favorite things. Now brainstorm for five minutes. Filling in the squares across the page, write down the first things you think of about your hero's looks. Do the same for the other categories. When you have finished, you will know 30 things about your hero. Some might be weird. Some you might discard. Some might trigger a whole new set of ideas.

The right name is like a password

Discovering your hero's name can sometimes bring him or her to life at once. If you're stuck trying to think of a name, try the lists in baby books or on the Internet, or flip through a telephone book. If you make up a name, say it out loud first to find out what it sounds like. Don't make it too complicated for readers to read. Leia, R2-D2, David, Lina, and Doon are simple but pleasing. They have a poetic ring.

LEIA   R2-D2   DOON   LINA

Give your hero problems and weaknesses

No one wants to read stories about people with perfect lives. Heroes need serious personal problems as well as some major external threat to overcome. In *Dream-Weaver*, Eth's major personal problem revolves around her cruel brother Liadd, but this story also weaves into a wider threat: Her planet is about to be colonized by greedy Earth settlers. Her strengths and weaknesses are played out between these two predicaments, adding drama and suspense.

Now it's your turn

Create a past for your hero

Think of yourself as your hero. In five minutes, write down everything you know about yourself and your recent past. But remember, when you come to put this sort of information into your story, you must be swift and brief.

TIPS AND TECHNIQUES

Start a "special words" list in your notebook. Write down any word that catches your imagination. You'll know where to look the next time you are stuck for a name. Use your own experiences and emotions to help you build your characters. Think about how you felt when something bad happened to you.

CREATE YOUR VILLAIN

In science fiction, your hero's main external enemy is likely to be some sort of disaster, but you need some enemy characters, too. They might be purely evil like Darth Vader, or their wickedness might not be so easy to spot.

Imagine the face of evil

First, think about what makes your villains so evil. Are they hungry for power? Do they want great wealth or some special knowledge that will help them control everyone or make them immortal? Are they simply cruel and get their pleasure from destroying things? Are they envious of your hero? Did they start off good and then turn to evil ways?

Now it's your turn

Know your villain

In a 10-minute practice, brainstorm your chief villain. What is his or her motivation? Think about your villain's weaknesses and how these might help the story. Repeat the exercise on page 22 with your villain as the focus.

TIPS AND TECHNIQUES

The more you question your villains, the more you'll find out about them and the more intriguing they'll become. Sometimes the most evil thing is something you can't quite see. The writer can reveal it indirectly through the fear in the characters' minds.

GETTING STARTED   SETTING THE SCENE   CHARACTERS   VIEWPOINT

Villainous Profiles

Here are some ideas for different types of villains:

HUMAN EVIL

In Louise Lawrence's Dream-Weaver, *Eth tries to make her brother Liadd less cruel by weaving him better dreams as he sleeps, but his psychic self wakes and attacks her.*

UNIVERSE DOMINATION

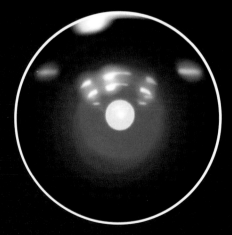

The most frightening thing about George Lucas' evil creation, Darth Vader, is that he was once an ordinary man. But with his cyborg implants and deadly pursuit of evil power, he has turned into a blood-chilling man-machine.

MONSTROUS PURSUERS

Greg Bear's main predator is the huge Death Eagle, who stalks the pages of Dinosaur Summer. *With its "scimitar beak," "knife-like teeth," and "black-feathered arms," it stops the readers' hearts whenever they hear its terrible cries across the jungle plateau.*

LURKING THREAT

Orson Scott Card hardly lets us see the bug-like invaders in Ender's Game. *We fear them because Ender himself is desperate to save his sister so they "won't split her skull with a beam so hot that her brains burst the skull."*

ALIENS ON EARTH

In The Day of the Triffids, *John Wyndham's aliens are 10-foot-tall walking plants that attack humanity.*

CYBER EVIL

In Arthur C. Clarke's 2001: A Space Odyssey, *the thinking, feeling computer HAL 9000 receives conflicting human messages and develops murderous inclinations toward the human crew of its spaceship.*

DEVELOP A SUPPORTING CAST

As in real life, your science-fiction heroes and villains will be judged by the company they keep. Scenes with minor characters are a good way to show readers what your main characters are really like. You can show them being mean or brave in scenes with someone else.

Create more characters

Minor characters won't be as developed as heroes and villains, but they must seem real. Base it on someone you know, or find a striking characteristic that brings them to life. For example, Marvin the android in Douglas Adams' *The Hitchhiker's Guide to the Galaxy* is always whining about being depressed. C-3PO in the Star Wars series may be clever, but he complains a lot and isn't very brave. When the little alien Beebo is around in the Alien Classmate series, you know that he is going to cause chaos.

In *Dinosaur Summer*, the young hero, Peter, is a thoughtful boy who is overshadowed by his adventurer father. But through his relationships with the captive dinosaurs, Greg Bear shows us that Peter has hidden strengths. He cares for them and risks his life for them, which also makes the reader care—about both Peter and his charges.

26

GETTING STARTED · · · · · · · · · · · · · · · · · · SETTING THE SCENE · · · · · · · · · CHARACTERS · · · · · · · · · VIEWPOINT

TIPS AND TECHNIQUES

The supporters of your hero or villain—whether spaceship crew or aliens— must help move your story forward. If they haven't a job to do, cut them out. Showing, not telling, is the key to exciting storytelling.

Magical companions

In the Jumpman series, Theodore Pine, the time-traveling boy from 3,000 years in the future, has a marvelous cyber-coat. Theo's dialogue with it throughout the story tells us both about his own world and about the kind of person he is, thus avoiding a lot of description. In the next excerpt, where a faulty jumpman has left Theo stranded in the 21st century, we soon see that he can't handle things going wrong:

"Atmosphere Report, Theodore, brought to you by Realfish. So Real You'll Think It Swam Over For Dinner! It's 23.8 degrees, barometer rising ... Occasional showers expected along the coast but overall—"

"Shut up," ordered Theo. "Shut up shut up shut up shut up," he kept on repeating a little hysterically. "You're about as useful as a moontan. A real Coat might be of some actual help here. I mean, have you noticed that we're visible?"

James Valentine, the Jumpman series

Now it's your turn

Picture your characters

In your next writing practice, try sketching your ideas. Ask your creations if they have special powers and how they will help or harm your hero. Jot down the answers beside the drawing. Hunt for good names. Make a list of possible ones and try them out for size in your mind.

CHOOSE A POINT OF VIEW

You have a story to tell, but before you can start, you must decide on your story's point of view. Do you want to tell the readers everything that is happening and show all the characters' views? Or do you want to tell one particular person's story?

The omniscient view

Most fantasy stories are written using the omniscient, or all-seeing, view. This means that the narrator can tell how the hero feels when he or she is trapped in an enchanted forest, and then switch to the wizard's lair to reveal what the wizard has planned for the hero. Science fiction is more often told from the point of view of the main character. This is called third-person viewpoint.

The third-person view

Third-person viewpoint is usually written in the past tense. You might write a few lines in your story like these: "Counselor Galt bowed briefly and turned on his heel. He knew he must not show his anger to these inferior beings. Humans! Let the universe be rid of their selfish, pigheaded thinking."

When writing from this limited viewpoint, you cannot suddenly switch and say what the humans thought of Galt— not unless Galt actually knows their opinion, in which case you might write something like this: "He knew the Earthlings didn't respect him or his Aurean people. He could see it in their eyes."

Multiple viewpoints

Short stories are usually written from one viewpoint, two at most. But in novels, there can be multiple viewpoints. This adds to the story's suspense and complexity. The Animorphs series has five alternating viewpoints; each chapter switches to one of the five main characters. The books are fast-paced and plot-driven—what is happening is more important than developing the characters. All the characters speak in the first person, which is an exciting point of view to use.

Now it's your turn

Write a scene

Take half an hour to write a short scene from your own story. Describe your hero battling with some villain. First write from the all-knowing viewpoint, describing what is happening on both sides as they fight. Then rewrite it in the third person past tense, giving only your hero's viewpoint. Finally, write it in the first person—as if you are the hero telling the story in your own words.

TIPS AND TECHNIQUES

The first-person viewpoint can make an extraordinary tale sound true. You could write your story as a starship log or a series of letters. You might be a human survivor of some disaster or a mad scientist documenting your experiments.

TELL YOUR STORY'S STORY

When your story starts bubbling fiercely in your mind, it's a good idea to write a few paragraphs about it. This brief account is called a synopsis and will help you keep your story on track. Write just enough to be intriguing, but don't give away the ending.

To get some ideas, look at the back covers of some sci-fi books and read the blurbs. See how they say just enough to whet your appetite: Do you simply have to findout what happens next? The blurb to Nicholas Fisk's *A Rag, a Bone and a Hank of Hair* conjures up a nightmarish vision of the future:

> *It's the end of the 22nd century. The birth-rate is falling. So the Government begins to manufacture Reborns—new people from old. Brin is chosen to monitor the Reborns. But how long can he keep them from discovering the truth about their existence ...*
> Nicholas Fisk, *A Rag, a Bone and a Hank of Hair*

The synopsis for *A Wrinkle in Time*, by Madeleine L'Engle, questions the possibility of traveling through space:

> *It is a dark and stormy night. Meg Murry, her small brother Charles Wallace, and their mother are in the kitchen for a midnight snack when a most disturbing visitor arrives. Meg's father had been experimenting with this fifth dimension of time travel when he mysteriously disappeared. Now the time has come for Meg, her friend Calvin, and Charles Wallace to rescue him. But can they outwit the forces of evil they will encounter on their heart-stopping journey through space?*
> Madeleine L'Engle, *A Wrinkle in Time*

Now it's your turn

Write your blurb

Sum up your story in a single striking sentence, then develop it in two or three short paragraphs. Think about your potential readers and try to draw them in to make them want to read the book.

Make a story map

You have a synopsis that says what your story is about. You have a cast of characters and a setting, and you know from whose viewpoint you wish to tell the tale. The last thing you need before you tell your tale is a story map.

Plan your story into scenes

Before filmmakers can start filming, they must know the main story episodes and decide how they can best tell their story in filmed images. To help them, they make a story map by outlining the plot (the sequence of events) in a series of sketches called storyboards. You can do this for your story. Draw the main episodes in pictures. Add notes saying what is happening in each scene.

TIPS AND TECHNIQUES

If you can't sum up your story simply, it might be too complicated, so simplify it. As you work on your own synopsis, start by asking yourself, "Whose story is this and how will I tell it?"

Think about your theme

When you think about your scenes, give some thought to your story's theme. In science fiction, this might be the end of civilization, the rights and wrongs of exploiting another life-form, what it means to be human, or what it would be like for an alien life-form on Earth, as is the case with the Superman stories.

Create a synopsis

Novelists often list all their chapters before they start writing and say briefly what will happen in each one. This is called a chapter synopsis. It stops them from losing track of the story once they start writing. *Gulliver's Adventures in Lilliput* is part of Jonathan Swift's four-part novel called *Gulliver's Travels*. It was published in 1726 and is now considered an early example of science fiction. There are a number of short story adaptations.

A famous example

Here are some possible storyboard captions for *Gulliver's Adventures in Lilliput*, written by Jonathan Swift.

1. Gulliver is shipwrecked and washes ashore.
2. He wakes up to find himself captured by Lilliputians.
3. He meets the emperor, and six Lilliputians shoot at him.
4. Gulliver's kindness to his attackers earns the emperor's favor.
5. Gulliver reviews the troops and learns of war with Blefuscu.
6. Gulliver saves Lilliput by dragging enemy ships there.
7. Gulliver refuses to destroy the enemy and is charged with treason.
8. Lilliputian courtiers plot against Gulliver, urging his death.
9. The emperor lessens the punishment to blinding, but Gulliver flees.
10. Gulliver finds a boat and escapes to sea, where he is rescued.

Now it's your turn

Weave a story web

In the middle of a large piece of paper, draw a rough sketch of your hero within a circle. As you are drawing, imagine that you are that hero, trying to decide which way to go. Think about the problems you have and what you are going to do about them. Draw six spokes around your hero circle. Each leads to another circle. Inside each one, sketch a different scene or write it as notes. Each circle will be some new course of action that you might take or some obstacle that an enemy sets in your path. Give yourself 20 minutes.

Novels versus short stories

Novels aren't short stories made longer, but short stories made deeper. They still have beginnings, middles, and ends, as well as heroes with problems and conflicts, but the main story is expanded with subplots and many more characters. Novels are usually divided into chapters, which also have beginnings, middles, and ends. Once you have worked out the main episodes, or scenes, in your story, you can decide if you are going to tell them briefly in a short story or develop each one further as a chapter for a novel.

Reducing a novel

To turn *Gulliver's Adventures in Lilliput* into a short story, the original novel's chapters are reduced to a few key scenes. These are then retold more simply. The tale works well as a shorter story. It has a hero with problems, some conflict in the middle, a climax, and a hopeful ending. It also has a good theme about the use and abuse of power.

TIPS AND TECHNIQUES

Don't let a novel's length discourage you from starting one. If you use the story map approach, it can be easier to write a novel than to write a good short story.

You have planned your plot and are ready to start telling your own story. It is time for blast-off. Focus on your hero. How will you win the readers to his or her cause? A good beginning is critical.

But where do you start your story?

Many stories start at the point when their heroes' lives are "normal." They may have their usual problems, but nothing much is happening. Then comes some crisis or external conflict that turns their lives upside down. Something has to be done about it. The advantage of doing this is that the readers can share the hero's shock when the crisis happens. Other stories leap straight into some powerful action that is so involving that the readers are instantly hooked. Only then will the writer pause to give some of the characters' back stories or histories, which will explain the opening scene.

TIPS AND TECHNIQUES

Story beginnings introduce the hero, reveal his or her problems, and start the quest to resolve them. Use your library to study opening sentences. Write down your favorites. Work on your own beginning sentence. Write it and rewrite it. Read it out loud.

Write your opening sentence

Once you have thought up a good opening scene that makes your hero seem really interesting, you must work out an attention-grabbing first sentence. Here are some good examples:

Make your character sympathetic

"Norby! What have you done to my computer terminal?" "I'm only trying to help, Jeff. I just inserted a program that will help you learn the Unified Field Theory for the second exam. If you'd paid attention to my teaching, you wouldn't have failed the first exam and delayed our departure for Izz."

Janet and Isaac Asimov, *Norby and the Court Jester*

Be dramatic or funny

It was a dark and stormy night. In her attic bedroom Margaret Murry, wrapped in an old patchwork quilt, sat on the foot of her bed and watched the trees tossing in the frenzied lashing of the wind. Behind the trees clouds scudded frantically across the sky. Every few moments the moon ripped through them, creating wraithlike shadows that raced along the ground.

Madeleine L'Engle, *A Wrinkle in Time*

Create mystery

Once the brontosaurus' small, slow brain realized the things were neither edible plants nor dangerous enemies, it forgot about them. And so it did not disturb the thing they left behind.

William Sleator, *The Green Futures of Tycho*

Stir strong emotions and be mysterious

"Mother!?" There was no reply. She hadn't expected one. Her mother had been dead now for four days, and Kira could tell that the last of the spirit was drifting away.

Lois Lowry, *Gathering Blue*

BUILD THE SUSPENSE

If story beginnings must be gripping, then middles should grip harder. From the first page, your story needs to build tension and suspense. If your story is drifting, try to see things through your characters' eyes.

Try a false happy ending

One good ploy to create suspense is to have a false happy ending.
For example, the hero seems to have saved the world from invasion, but just when everyone is celebrating, a more deadly alien force appears on
the planet's radar. This gives the writer the chance to build up
the excitement on an even bigger scale.

Maintain the action

Plenty of activity also holds readers' interests. Keep your
characters engaged with their quest at all times—on the move,
working things out, coming to the wrong conclusions,
having fights, or escaping disasters.

Make your heroes time-challenged

If your heroes are time-challenged, this
instantly adds drama. Will Ender
(*Ender's Game*) be trained in time to
destroy the next alien fleet? Will Eth
(*Dream-Weaver*) learn what she needs
to know before the unwanted
spacecraft lands on her planet? Will
Lina and Doon (*The City of
Ember*) solve the problems of
their dying city before the
lights go out forever?

Now it's your turn

Find strength in weakness

Focus on your hero's flaws or weaknesses. In five minutes, write your first thoughts on how these might complicate and add drama to your story. Do the same for any other main characters. Perhaps your hero has unusual fears or physical problems. Perhaps your hero's friend turns out to have doubtful motives. Think how these factors might bring your story to a climax.

Create more challenges

Don't forget to stir in complications and pile on the challenges. If your hero has been pursued by some bully or aggressor, make the reader think the bad guy has found a new target. Then let the villain return with some worse torment. This time, your hero must deal with this situation once and for all. The questions of how the hero decides to do this and whether his or her plan will work add some new suspense. Your hero's weaknesses could come into play, too. Keep piling up problems to make your story more exciting.

TIPS AND TECHNIQUES

Action scenes should spring from the characters' own plans, not from your need to revive a lagging story. But when you do include them, make them as exciting as possible. Your characters' weaknesses can add more twists and turns to the story.

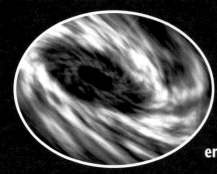

Finding a good ending is perhaps the hardest part of storytelling. Some writers like to think up their exact ending before they start writing. Others don't want to know the ending until they get there.

Resolve all the problems

As you plan your ending, think again about problems, conflict, and resolution. Good endings must bring the hero's problems and conflicts (plot) to a climax and then resolve them in satisfying ways. The ending should also refer to the story's beginning, reminding readers that something important has changed in the course of the story (such as, the hero has overcome some weakness).

Intriguing endings

Most readers like some sort of happy ending, but don't be predictable. In science fiction, the endings may create mixed feelings. Your heroes might have overcome some enemy and learned or gained something, but they may also have lost something or had to make some sacrifices. So rather than a simple and happy ending, make it hopeful instead. In *Return of the Jedi*, when Luke Skywalker refuses to be lured to the dark side, Emperor Palpatine turns all his evil against him. Seeing his son being destroyed, Darth Vader destroys Palpatine but is wounded himself. Before he dies, he asks Luke to remove the mask. He dies as Anakin Skywalker and not the monster he had become. For Luke, this ending is desperately hard, gaining and losing his father all at once, but the forces of good have been saved.

Now it's your turn

Choose your own ending

Read the ending of your favorite sci-fi story. Can you think of an alternative ending?
See if you can write it, then put it aside. Go back and read both versions later.
Now, which ending do you prefer and why?

A twist in the tale

Many sci-fi stories have twist-in-the-tale endings. All along,
you've been assuming the enemy is an alien, but then you find
out the humans are more dangerous. Or maybe an android
turns out to have more humanity than its heartless
human creator. To do this successfully, you need to
drop subtle clues throughout your story. This is called
foreshadowing. The reader will be surprised by the
twist but will then think, "I should have known."

Bad endings are ones that

- fizzle out because you've run out of ideas

- rely on some coincidence or surprise twist that hasn't
  been mentioned or set up earlier in the story

- fail to show how the characters have changed in some way

- are too grim and depressing and leave the reader with no hope

TIPS AND TECHNIQUES

*Don't forget to look at your story map,
if you are stuck. Or brainstorm your
hero in a circle again (see page 33).*

MAKE YOUR WORDS WORK

Words are valuable things. Every one you use should enhance your story in some way. Readers can enjoy your thrilling story so much more if it is free from rambling sentences and too many adjectives.

Use vivid imagery

If you can sum up scenes in images that trigger the senses, it is like adding special effects to your story. Try using metaphors and similes to bring your story to life. These are word pictures. A metaphor is when you call a man a mouse, meaning that he is scared. A simile is a comparison: as quiet as a mouse.

Choose striking verbs, too. In the Greg Bear example below, one-syllable verbs like "dropped" and "thrust" are good action words that echo the activity. The simile—"like a truckload of knives"—is stunning. It knocks the breath out of you.

> *And the death eagle dropped on her like a truckload of knives. Its white-gorgeted griffin's head thrust again and again, beak stripping skin into ribbons, shredding tendons.*
>
> Greg Bear, *Dinosaur Summer*

Change the rhythm and length of your sentences

This is another way to keep readers reading. Like in the Greg Bear example on the previous page, action scenes need short, sharp phrases that focus exactly on what is happening. But if you are building up for something scary, you can spin out longer phrases, adding sharp details that make the scene real. Imagine yourself creeping up on your reader. Then strike!

Change the mood

Changes in mood will also give your story edge. Science fiction often deals with catastrophes, but if your story is gloomy from start to finish, no one will want to read it. Amid mounting tension, some humor can give readers light relief. Or if your story is humorous, try to give it some serious angles, too. In the same way, readers also need a break from action sequences. This lets your readers catch their breath and allows the dust to settle before the story moves on.

Now it's your turn

Use words effectively

To give your writing bite, exercise your word-choosing skills. Brainstorm more lists: How many words for "flying" can you think of? How many words for "shine"? Reinvent sayings: The cliché "as white as snow" could become "as white as a snow goose's tail, a cannibal's smile, or an Alaskan snowdrift." Read the dictionary. Play word games.

TIPS AND TECHNIQUES

Remember that your characters will have different moods, too. Use them. Try ending a dramatic scene on a cliffhanger. Leave your heroes in peril and drive your readers to find out what happens next.

USE DRAMATIC DIALOGUE

Dialogue lets readers hear your characters' own voices. Whether they are an alien or some human from the future, they must sound just right. Dialogue adds color, pace, mood, and suspense to your story.

Let your characters speak for themselves

The best way to learn about dialogue is to switch on your listening ear and eavesdrop. Tune in to the way people phrase their words. Write down any good idioms—someone saying "hit the road" or "shove off" instead of "go away." Watch people's body language when they are whispering or arguing. Look, listen, and absorb.

Now it's your turn

The art of writing good dialogue

Tune in to a TV talk show. Spend 10 minutes writing down exactly what people say—including all the ums, ers, and repetitions. Listen for a range of voices: young, old, smart, foolish, angry, or cheery. Next compare it to some dialogue in a book. You will see at once that written dialogue does not include all the hesitations of natural speech, but it gives an edited impression of how people speak to one another. Fictional dialogue should mimic real speech, but it should not match real speech.

TIPS AND TECHNIQUES

When writing dialogue, stick to "he said" or "she said" for your tags most of the time, but use words like "asked," "cried," or "whispered" to create some variety or to suit the situation in your story.

Following convention

The way dialogue is written down follows conventions. It is usual to start a new paragraph with every new speaker. What they say is enclosed in quotation marks, followed by "he said" or "she said" to indicate the speaker. In this example (right), notice that speech tags are left out in an exchange between Peter and his father when it is clear who is speaking. Simple speech verbs like "said" and "asked" are repeated and are not cluttered with adverbs such as "loudly," "quietly," or "angrily." If you read the passage out loud, you will find it has a good rhythmic flow that makes it easy to follow.

> *"I have a confession to make."* Peter narrowed his eyes.
> *"What sort of confession?"*
> *"I got a telegram from your mother. Last week. I didn't bother to tell you—"*
> *"Why?"* Peter asked.
> *"It was addressed to me."* Anthony returned to the front room and pulled the crumpled piece of paper from his shirt pocket. *"She's worried about you. Summer's here. She thinks you're going to catch polio from all these crowds. She forbids you to swim in municipal pools."*
> Peter had hoped his mother might have sent a message inviting him to come to Chicago for a visit.
> *"Oh,"* he said.

Greg Bear, *Dinosaur Summer*

Now it's your turn

Write a good argument

Remember an argument you had or heard. Write it in a dialogue. Fictionalize it and change the names, but pour anger into the words. Don't rely on tags like "yelled" or "screamed" to show the mood. When you have finished, read it out loud. Revise it by taking out any unnecessary "saids" and cutting down all the spoken words to a minimum. You are learning the art of editing your own work.

USE DRAMATIC DIALOGUE

Dialogue: Why do we need it?

Dialogue breaks up the blocks of narrative (storytelling) and gives the reader's eyes a rest. It increases the pace, because it is quicker to read and is a direct way of giving readers information.

Think about the viewpoint

If you are telling your story through one character's eyes, you can only give that character's opinions, thoughts, and observations. They can't *know* what others are thinking and feeling. Dialogue lets readers hear other characters' views directly. For example, Greg Bear's exchange between Peter and Anthony (on the previous page) is written from Peter's viewpoint. We watch Anthony through Peter's eyes and hear what Peter hears. We don't know what Anthony is thinking.

Move the story forward

Dialogue is a key way to move the story forward. Characters do not make idle chitchat. Whatever they say will convey information—about themselves, other characters, and what is happening. You can use it to reveal their history or to drop hints that foreshadow dangers ahead. You can show characters lying and misleading other characters. Or you can make characters give themselves away.

Provoking emotions

Remember the *Dinosaur Summer* extract on the previous page? The author, Greg Bear (left), says a lot about the characters. He tells us about Peter's life and his relationship with his mother. If you tried to write all this information as a piece of narrative, it would probably be three times as long. Peter's short answers also suggest caution learned from experience. There is a hint of Anthony's contempt for his ex-wife's meddling. But it's Peter's sad little "oh" that makes us sympathize with him.

Now it's your turn

Talk with the enemy

Write a short piece of dialogue between a human and an alien. One of them is pleading for his life. Decide whose point of view you are writing from. Try to find ways of indicating why one wants to exterminate the other. Make it humorous, if you want to. Try to make the characters sound different from each other—an alien will not have the same speech patterns as a human, even if they are speaking a common language. When you have finished, write the same thing as a piece of straight narrative, including the same information. Which version is more interesting to read?

Let your characters sound different from you

It is tempting to devise very strange words for your alien characters to speak by using strings of consonants or odd punctuation. Avoid doing this. It is difficult for the reader's eye to unravel, and if readers keep stumbling over strange words, they will stop reading. Your story will have failed, no matter how good it was otherwise.

Suggest language difference

You can make your characters sound different by small touches done sparingly. Devise a greeting, such as Mr. Spock's "Live long and prosper" in *Star Trek* or some catchwords or phrases that occur naturally in their remarks. Non-native English speakers often speak in a more formal way. Compare "It's my arm! You broke it!" to "It is my arm! You have broken it!"

Now it's your turn

Family talk

Write down a typical conversation between you and one of your parents. Try to capture exactly how your parent speaks. What words or phrases do they habitually use that are different from yours? Rewrite it with a grandparent or elderly aunt speaking. Are there more differences?

Invented language

There are, of course, always writers who push the boundaries. Ursula K. Le Guin uses her upbringing in Indian cultures and the knowledge of several languages to create a mythic way of speaking for the characters of her imagined worlds.

Accents

In Douglas Adams' *Hitchhiker's Guide to the Galaxy*, the two-headed Zaphod's hip way of speaking is caught in the following exchange: "Hey Earthman? You hungry kid?" said Zaphod's voice.

Stay in character

In *The Hitchhiker's Guide to the Galaxy*, Marvin the Paranoid Android has such a well-drawn character that you always know when he is speaking—usually mournfully.

"You think you've got problems," said Marvin as if he was addressing a newly occupied coffin, "what are you to do if you are a manically depressed robot? No, don't bother to answer that, I'm fifty thousand times more intelligent than you and even I don't know the answer. It gives me a headache just trying to think down to your level."

Douglas Adams, *The Hitchhiker's Guide to the Galaxy*

TIPS AND TECHNIQUES

Dialogue will reveal lots of differences between the speakers, such as age, education, intelligence, and where they are from. It will also give clues to the speakers' relationship (such as whether they are friends or foes). Listen, listen, listen.

BEAT WRITER'S BLOCK

Learning to write has ups and downs, and even famous writers get stuck. This is called writer's block. If you have been sticking to the writer's golden rule (sitting down and writing regularly), then you already have some weapons to fight writer's block.

Think positively about what you have written

Whenever your internal critic looms on your brain, do a timed brainstorming exercise to cut it down to size. Write something positive, perhaps about your favorite things or a great moment in your life. The more you do this, the more you will build up your writer's power—just like Luke Skywalker learned to wield his light saber.

Make it a habit

To be a writer, you must learn the writing habit. Write regularly—letters, e-mails, diary entries—and learn to write when you don't feel like it. Whenever you do a timed brainstorming session—even if it is only two minutes—you prove you can write.

Cope with criticism

No one enjoys rejection or criticism, but they are important parts of learning to be a writer. If you invite someone to read your stories, you have to prepare yourself for negative comments. As you develop your writing skills, you will add faith in yourself and your storytelling skills. Try to see criticism as a chance to make your story better.

GETTING STARTED · · · · · · · · · SETTING THE SCENE · · · · · · CHARACTERS · · · · · · VIEWPOINT

Now it's your turn

Think positively

Write on the cover of your notebook: Writing is out of this world, but it's not always easy!

Now brainstorm for five minutes, listing all the things you find difficult about writing. Repeat the exercise, only this time list all the things you love about writing. Now look over the problems. Are these things that can be fixed with more time, practice, and reading? Is learning to write more important to you than the problems? If the answer is yes, then give yourself a gold star. You are still heading toward a successful mission.

Find new ideas

There are other causes of writer's block. One is believing that you have nothing to write about. But now you know that ideas are everywhere. The trick is to stop panicking and sit quietly. Any of the exercises in this book could help you find some new ideas. Or watch your favorite sci-fi shows. Don't try to copy them—that would be plagiarism—but use the plots or characters to inspire ideas of your own.

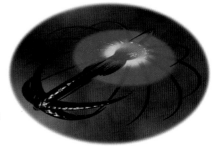

Get past halfway

Getting stuck halfway through your story can be very depressing, but if it happens, it is often because you haven't thought the story out fully. Some vital ingredient is missing, and the best way to find it is to go back to your story map (see page 31). Or simply leave this story for a while and start something new. All stories take their natural time to emerge.

The kind of writer's block that leaves you stuck usually means you have not done enough planning. If you have been following the exercises, you will already know how to escape some of these black holes. Here are some more strategies:

Stir your imagination

One way to sort out a story block is to play the what-if game. Remember the "What if I'm an android" exercise on page 15? Try asking some new questions to help you create this character in more detail. For example, what if I confided in my best friend? What if he or she told my secret to someone else, and the whole school discovered it? What if they all turned against me? See how the questions build into a possible storyline.

Build character

If your key character isn't coming to life, turn your writing problem into a game with friends or family. You'll need a large sheet of paper. Sit in a circle, and in two minutes, write a brief description of your hero at the top of the paper. Pass it on, and let the next person add his or her thoughts to yours and so on around the circle. When the suggestions return to you, you may see your hero in a whole new light.

Write as a group

Try composing a group story. Have 12 or more scraps of paper. Write a character idea on each one and drop them into a hat. Everyone chooses a character randomly and must be responsible for developing that character and weaving it into the story. Take turns making story suggestions. There are two rules: Speak your first thoughts, and don't mind if others improve on your ideas. The end result should be like a chapter synopsis.

Keep a diary

If you run out of things to write, start a diary. Write about life at school or home, recording all the details of your hobbies and interests. Set yourself a minimum target for each entry, like 300 words or half a page. If you use a computer for writing, you can count the words easily. That way you can prove that you are working really hard.

Now it's your turn

Break down resistance

If you still think you have absolutely nothing to say, try this. Give yourself 10 minutes to describe the most boring, mind-numbing thing you can think of. Say exactly why you find it boring in the most telling words possible. Say how you survived the experience. Or maybe you didn't. Maybe it turned you into some other life-form that just pretends to be you. Be funny, dramatic, or downright ridiculous. Write it to entertain your friends.

TIPS AND TECHNIQUES

You won't run out of ideas if you keep reading, but remember to write them down in your notebook. If all else fails, walk the dog or clean your bedroom. Doing tasks that give your mind a rest could be just the way to spring an idea.

TAKE THE NEXT STEP

Finishing your first story is a wonderful achievement. You have created something entirely new, proven you can write, and probably learned a lot about yourself, too. So put your story aside for a week or so and start a new one.

Give it a rest

You've worked long and hard to finish your story, so it's time for you to take a rest. Putting it aside will make it easier to spot flaws and read it with fresh eyes when you read it again later. All writers can continue to improve their stories if they are able to step back and read it as if they were someone reading it for the first time.

Another story?

Perhaps while you were writing the first story, another idea started simmering in your mind. Perhaps you made a few mental notes. Do those ideas still excite you? Go back to the start of this book and repeat some of the brainstorming exercises to help you develop the idea further. The Star Trek and Norby series have a complete adventure in each book, but the details of the main characters' lives run on from book to book to keep the readers hooked.

How about a sequel?

When thinking about your next work, ask yourself: "Can I write a sequel and develop the story? Is there a minor character whose tale I'm burning to tell?" Science-fiction stories lend themselves to sequels and series, because the effort that goes into creating a speculative world is bound to lead to more ideas. Or what about writing a trilogy? These three-book stories mirror the beginning-middle-end principle of a single story structure—but on a grander scale. Book one introduces the characters and their problems, book two develops the conflict, and book three has the climax and resolution of the story.

A famous example

At the end of *The Lost Years* in the Star Trek series, J. M. Dillard finishes with the sad parting between Dr. McCoy and Spock but, at the very last moment, manages to slip in a hopeful little hint that could suggest more stories to come:

> *McCoy stood, surprised by the sudden tightness of his throat. "Goodbye, Spock. Take care." He watched as the Vulcan, a stark and lonely figure in black, walked out of the empty bar. And somehow, his heart refused to accept that this time was the last.*
>
> J. M. Dillard, *The Lost Years*

You can learn a great deal from hearing how successful writers came to write. Most writers will tell you that it took a long time and that they wrote a lot of rubbish at first. They would also add that they never stop learning their craft.

So if it's not easy, why do writers write?

- They write because they must.

- They write to tell a story that must be told.

- They write because they believe that nothing is more important than stories.

- They write because it's the thing they want to do most. In short, it's a passion.

Terry Pratchett

Famous for his Discworld books, Terry Pratchett published his first sci-fi story in his school magazine when he was 13. Two years later, he was published professionally in the magazine *Science Fantasy*. He says this:

"We're living in science fiction, but we don't realize it. I was buying something for my wife in Perth, Australia, last time I was on tour. I couldn't remember her size, so I phoned her up. ... That is a science fiction conversation! All the more so for being mundane. I'm actually making a phone call all around the world on my mobile phone, to ask my wife her dress size!"

L. Frank Baum

Although L. Frank Baum was not a sci-fi writer—he wrote *The Wizard of Oz*—what he had to say about writing is true of science fiction:

"Imagination has given us the steam engine, the telephone, the talking machine, and the automobile, for these things had to be dreamed of before they became realities. So I believe that dreams—day dreams ... with your eyes wide open ... are likely to lead to the betterment of the world."

Ursula K. Le Guin

Ursula K. Le Guin advises young writers to care about what words mean and how they use them. She wrote her first time-travel story when she was 10 years old, but when she failed to publish it, she stopped writing and spent the next nine years reading. She says:

"Science fiction begins at the moment where science ends, and then you go on and build on what is known.

Read and read the best. One doesn't have to have scientific knowledge. ... If I need to know anything for my story, I go to the library and read about it. I think most science-fiction writers work this way."

TIPS AND TECHNIQUES

Science fiction can sometimes become science fact. Writing stories and inventing things both begin in the human imagination.

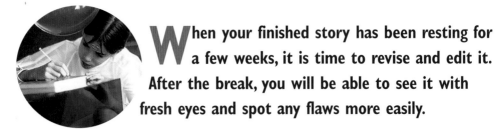

When your finished story has been resting for a few weeks, it is time to revise and edit it. After the break, you will be able to see it with fresh eyes and spot any flaws more easily.

Edit your work

Reading your work aloud will help you to simplify rambling sentences and correct dialogue that doesn't flow. Cut out all unnecessary adjectives and adverbs and extra words like "very" and "really." This will instantly make your writing crisper. Think about the story, too. Does it have a satisfying end? Has the hero resolved his or her problem in the best way? Does the end link with the beginning, and has your hero learned something and changed? When your story is as good as can be, write it out again or type it up on a computer. This is your manuscript.

Think of a title

It is important to think up a good title; choose something intriguing and eye-catching. Think about some titles you know and like.

Be professional

If you are sending your manuscript to a publisher, magazine, or agent, it's best to type it up. Manuscripts should always be printed on one side of plain white paper with double spacing. Pages should be numbered, and new chapters should start

a new page. You can include your title as a header on the top of each page. At the front, have a title page that gives your name, address, telephone number, and e-mail address.

Make your own book

If your school has its own computer lab, why not use it to publish your own story or to make a story anthology, or collection? A computer will let you choose your own font (print style) or justify the text (make even margins like a professionally printed page). When you have

typed and saved your story to a file, you can edit it quickly with the spelling and grammar checker. You can also move sections of your story around with the cut-and-paste tool, which saves a lot of rewriting. Having your story on a computer file also means you can print a copy whenever you need one, or you can revise the whole story, if you want to.

Design a cover

Once your story is in good shape, you can print it and then use the computer to design the cover. A graphics program will let you scan and print your own artwork or download ready-made graphics. You could also use your own digital photographs and learn how to manipulate them to produce some highly original images. You can use yourself or your friends as models for your story's heroes.

TIPS AND TECHNIQUES

Whether you write your story on a computer or by hand, always make a copy before you give it to others to read. Otherwise, if they lose it, you will have lost all your precious work.

The next step is to find an audience to read your science-fiction story. Family members or classmates may be receptive. If you are really ambitious, you may want to get your work published via a publishing house or online site.

Some places to publish your story

There are several magazines and a number of writing Web sites that accept stories and novel chapters from young science-fiction writers. Some give writing advice. Several run regular competitions. Each site has its own rules about submitting work, so make sure you read carefully before you send in a story. You can also:

• Send stories to your school newspaper.
  If your school doesn't have a newspaper, start your own with like-minded friends.

• Keep your eyes peeled when reading your local newspaper or magazines. They might be running a writing competition you could enter.

• Check with local museums and colleges. Some run creative-writing workshops during school holidays.

Writing clubs

Starting a writing club or critique group and exchanging stories is a great way of getting your science-fiction story out there. It will also get you used to criticism from others, which will prove invaluable in learning how to write. Your local library might be kind enough to provide a space for such a club.

Case study

Ursula K. Le Guin's award-winning book, *The Left Hand of Darkness,* was rejected by an editor as being "unreadable" and the action "hopelessly bogged down." Le Guin now posts the message on her Web site as an encouragement to other writers who have received rejection letters. Her advice: "Hang in there!"

Find a book publisher

Secure any submission with a paper clip, and always enclose a short letter (saying what you have sent) and a stamped, self-addressed envelope for the story's return. Study the market and find out which publishing houses are most likely to publish science fiction. Addresses of publishing houses and information about whether they accept submissions can be found in writers' handbooks. Bear in mind that manuscripts that haven't been asked for or paid for by a publisher—unsolicited submissions—are rarely published.

Writer's tip

If your story is rejected by an editor, don't despair. See it as a chance to make the story better, and try again. Remember, having your work published is wonderful, but it is not the only thing. Being able to make up stories is a gift, so why not give yours to someone you love? Read it to a younger brother or sister. Tell it to your grandfather. Find your audience.

Some last words

Through stories, we can explore all the good and bad things that make us human. This is what good storytelling is about. It gives us hope. It shows us new possibilities. It sends us off on unknown and exciting missions.

Read! Write!

If you do, you'll head for the stars.

GLOSSARY

analogy—suggesting similarities between one thing (or situation) and another quite different thing (or situation)

back story—the history of characters and events that happened before the story begins

blurb—publisher's description on a book jacket that persuades you to read the book

chapter synopsis—an outline that describes briefly what happens in each chapter

cliffhanger—ending of a chapter or scene of a story at a nail-biting moment

editing—removing all unnecessary words from your story, correcting errors, and rewriting the text until the story is the best it can be

editor—the person at a publishing house who finds new books to publish and advises authors on how to improve their stories by telling them what needs to be added or cut

first-person viewpoint—a viewpoint that allows a single character to tell the story as if he or she had written it; readers feel as if that character is talking directly to them; for example: "It was July when I left for Timbuktu. Just the thought of going back there made my heart sing."

foreshadowing—dropping hints of coming events or dangers that are essential to the outcome of the story

genre—a particular type of fiction, such as fantasy, historical, adventure, mystery, science, or realistic

internal critic—the voice in your mind that constantly picks holes in your work and makes you want to give up

manuscript—your story when it is written down, either typed or by hand

metaphor—calling a man "a mouse" is a metaphor, a word picture; from it we learn in one word that the man is timid or weak, not that he is actually a mouse

motivation—the reason why a character does something

narrative—the telling of a story

omniscient viewpoint—an all-seeing narrator that sees all the characters and tells readers how they are acting and feeling

plagiarism—copying someone else's work and passing it off as your own; it is a serious offense

plot—the sequence of events that drives a story forward; the problems that the hero must resolve

point of view—the eyes through which a story is told

publisher—a person or company who pays for an author's manuscript to be printed as a book and who distributes and sells that book

sequel—a story that carries an existing one forward

simile—saying something is like something else, a word picture, such as "clouds like frayed lace"

speculative fiction—science fiction and fantasy that set stories in imagined worlds

synopsis—a short summary that describes what a story is about and introduces the main characters

theme—the main idea behind your story, such as overcoming a weakness, the importance of friendship, or good versus evil; a story can have more than one theme

third-person viewpoint—a viewpoint that describes the events of the story through a single character's eyes, such as "Jem's heart leaped in his throat. He'd been dreading this moment for months."

unsolicited submission—a manuscript that is sent to a publisher without being requested; these submissions usually end up in the "slush pile," where they may wait a long time to be read

writer's block—when writers think they can no longer write or have used up all their ideas

FURTHER INFORMATION

Visit your local libraries and make friends with the librarians. They can direct you to useful sources of information, including magazines that publish young people's short fiction. You can learn your craft and read great stories at the same time. Librarians will also know if any published authors are scheduled to speak in your area.

Many authors visit schools and offer writing workshops. Ask your teacher to invite a favorite author to speak at your school.

On the Web

For more information on this topic, use FactHound.
1. Go to *www.facthound.com*
2. Type in this book ID: 0756516439
3. Click on the *Fetch It* button.
FactHound will find the best Web sites for you.

Read more science fiction

Applegate, K.A. *The Arrival,* Animorphs. Milwaukee, Wis: Gareth Stevens, 2001.

Bear, Greg. *Dinosaur Summer.* New York: Aspect, 1998.

Card, Orson Scott. *Ender's Game.* New York: Starscape, 2002.

Clements, Andrew. *Things Not Seen.* New York: Philomel Books, 2002.

Conly, Jane Leslie. *The Rudest Alien on Earth.* New York: Henry Holt, 2002.

DuPrau, Jeanne. *The City of Ember.* New York: Random House, 2003.

DuPrau, Jeanne. *The People of Sparks.* New York: Random House, 2004.

Lawrence, Louise. *Dream-Weaver.* New York: Clarion Books, 1996.

L'Engle, Madeleine. *A Wrinkle in Time.* New York: Yearling, 2005.

Lowry, Lois. *Gathering Blue.* Boston: Houghton Mifflin, 2000.

Pratchett, Terry. *The Color of Magic: A Novel of Discworld.* New York: Harper, 2005.

Sleator, William. *The Green Futures of Tycho.* New York: Puffin Books, 1991.

Valentine, James. *Jumpman Rule #1: Don't Touch Anything.* New York: Simon & Schuster Books for Young Readers, 2005.

Waugh, Sylvia. *Earthborn.* New York: Delacorte Press, 2002.

Read all the Write Your Own books:

Write Your Own Adventure Story
ISBN: 0-7565-1638-2

Write Your Own Fantasy Story
ISBN: 0-7565-1639-0

Write Your Own Historical Fiction Story
ISBN: 0-7565-1640-4

Write Your Own Mystery Story
ISBN: 0-7565-1641-2

Write Your Own Realistic Fiction Story
ISBN: 0-7565-1642-0

Write Your Own Science Fiction Story
ISBN: 0-7565-1643-9

INDEX

Picture Credits: Art Archive: 8b, 9t, 10t & b, 18-19c, 24t, 41t, 43b, 51t, 57cl, 23b, 32t 33 all, 38-39c, 39b, 57t, 58t, 58b. Bettmann/Corbis: 46b. Corbis RF: 6-7 all, 12 all, 14-15 all, 16t, 17b, 29t, 30 all, 34c, 35t, 40t. Creatas: 4t, 19t, 28t, 42-43c, 48t, 49t, 52t, 54 all, 58b. Fotosearch: 16-17c, 30-31c, 43b, 44t, 50t, 56t and b. NASA: 8t, 18t, 59b. Rex Features: 1, 5t, 9b, 10-11c, 13 all, 17t, 20-21 all, 22 all, 23t, 24b, 25 all, 26-27 all, 28t, 29t, 32c, 36-37 all, 38b, 40t, 42t, 44b, 45, 48-49c, 50c, 51c, 52b, 53c and 53r, 55 all, 59tr, 60. Science Photo Library: 38t, 41b, 49b.

NOV 0 8 2008		
NOV 0 2 REC'D		
OCT 1 2 2011		
DEC 1 0 2011		
GAYLORD		PRINTED IN U.S.A.